TIME TRAVEL GUIDES

ANCIENT EGYPT

Liz Gogerly

Raintree

Chicago, Illinois

Designed by Steve Mead and Geoff Ward
Photo research by Ruth Blair
Illustrations by Eikon Illustration & Tim Slade
Printed by South China Printing Company Limited

11 10 09 08 07
10 9 8 7 6 5 4 3 2 1

Library of Congress Cataloging-in-Publication Data
Gogerly, Liz.
  Ancient Egypt / Liz Gogerly.
     p. cm. – (Time travel guides)
  Includes bibliographical references and index.
  ISBN-13: 978-1-4109-2728-6 (library binding -
hardcover)
  ISBN-10: 1-4109-2728-8 (library binding - hardcover)
  ISBN-13: 978-1-4109-2735-4 (pbk.)
  ISBN-10: 1-4109-2735-0 (pbk.)
1. Egypt–Civilization–To 332 B.C.–Juvenile literature. 2.
Egypt–Guidebooks–Juvenile literature. I. Title.
  DT61.G566 2007
  932–dc22
                              2006033959

Acknowledgments
The publishers would like to thank the following for
permission to reproduce photographs:
AKG Images **pp. 58–59** (Archives CDA; Guillot), **11,
54–55** (Erich Lessing), **6–7** (Herve Champollion), **41**
(Suzanne Held); Alamy **p. 34** (Gary Cook); Ancient Art
& Architecture Collection Ltd. **pp. 44–45** (Mary Jelliffe),
25 (Ronald Sheridan), **12** (Y. Shishido), **23, 38, 39, 40,
48–49**; Art Archive **pp. 36** (Bibliothèque Musée du
Louvre/Dagli Orti), **42–43** (British Museum, London/
Dagli Orti), **9, 20, 29, 37, 40, 47** (Egyptian Museum,
Cairo/Dagli Orti), **13, 14, 18–19, 21, 28, 46, 53** (Dagli
Orti), **58–59** (Egyptian Museum, Turin/Dagli Orti), **16**
(Khawam Collection, Paris/Dagli Orti), **15, 17, 21, 22,
30, 44** (Musée du Louvre, Paris/Dagli Orti), **51** (Ragab
Papyrus Institute, Cairo/Dagli Orti), **32–33**; Corbis pp.
26–27 (Frans Lemmens/Zefa), **31** (Jose Fuste Raga).

Cover images of a necklace with winged scarab pectoral
from Tutenkhamun's treasure, and Cuff bracelet
with eye Oudjat from the tomb of Sheshonq II, 930
BCE, reproduced with permission of Ancient Art &
Architecture Collection Ltd. Cover photograph of the
Sphinx reproduced with permission of Getty Images/
Photodisc.

The publishers would like to thank Christina Riggs for her
assistance in the preparation of this book.

Every effort has been made to contact copyright holders
of any material reproduced in this book. Any omissions
will be rectified in subsequent printings if notice is given
to the publishers.

Disclaimer
All the Internet addresses (URLs) given in this book were
valid at the time of going to press. However, due to the
dynamic nature of the Internet, some addresses may
have changed, or sites may have changed or ceased to
exist since publication. While the author and publishers
regret any inconvenience this may cause readers, no
responsibility for any such changes can be accepted by
either the author or the publishers

CONTENTS

Words that appear in the text in bold, **like this**, are explained in the Glossary.

MEDITERRANEAN SEA

N
W E
S

WESTERN DESERT

Alexandria

NILE DELTA

Giza **Memphis**
Saqqara

Herakleopolis

NILE RIVER

SPHINX AND
GREAT PYRAMIDS

Abydos

Thebes

Dahamsha

Hierakonpolis

Philae
Aswan

VALLEY OF THE KINGS

TEMPLE OF KARNAK

DEAD SEA

MAP OF ANCIENT EGYPT

Europe

Mediterranean Sea

EGYPT —

Africa

Indian
Ocean

SINAI PENINSULA

These are the amazing pyramids at Giza. Khufu's Great Pyramid is the biggest stone structure in the world.

CHAPTER 1

FACTS ABOUT ANCIENT EGYPT

Ancient Egypt is like no other place on Earth, so it is best to plan your trip well. You will be fascinated by the pyramids and tombs that are burial sites for pharaohs. The weather is often very hot and dry, but seek out the shade and you will be rewarded with a trip of a lifetime.

This section helps you find the best times to visit and tells you when you should avoid going. As well as information about the weather, you will find out about the politics, culture, and beliefs of the people who live in this intriguing ancient country.

WHEN TO TRAVEL

Ancient Egypt has a long and colorful history, spanning more than 3,000 years. Its history is divided into major periods, and then into dynasties. A dynasty is typically the time that one family or group of pharaohs (kings) ruled ancient Egypt.

TIMELINE OF ANCIENT EGYPT

(Note: dates given are approximate.)

EARLY DYNASTIC PERIOD (3100–2686 BCE)
1st dynasty
    Narmer (3100 BCE)

OLD KINGDOM (2686–2181 BCE)
4th dynasty
    Khufu (2589–2566 BCE)
    Khafre (2558–2532 BCE)

FIRST INTERMEDIATE PERIOD (2181–2055 BCE)

MIDDLE KINGDOM (2055–1650 BCE)
11th dynasty
    Mentuhotep II (2055–2004 BCE)

SECOND INTERMEDIATE PERIOD (1650–1550 BCE)

NEW KINGDOM (1550–1069 BCE)
18th dynasty
    Amenhotep II (1427–1400 BCE)
    Ramesses II (1279–1213 BCE)

THIRD INTERMEDIATE PERIOD (1069–747 BCE)

Key:
    Stay away
    Okay times to visit
    Best times to visit

EARLY TIMES

A good time to visit is during the early dynastic period, when Egypt becomes a united country for the first time. King Narmer (sometimes known as Menes) of Upper Egypt has just defeated the ruler of Lower Egypt. Narmer is the founder of the first dynasty of ancient Egyptian rulers.

OLD KINGDOM

Arrive during the Old Kingdom and you should head for the center of power in Memphis. Complete your trip with a day at the great pyramids of Khufu and Khafre at Giza.

MIDDLE KINGDOM

If you're looking for peace and quiet, try to plan your trip for the final years of the reign of Mentuhotep II. After years of civil war, he has brought peace back to ancient Egypt and is building an amazing temple just below the cliffs at Deir el-Bahri near the **capital** Thebes.

NEW KINGDOM

During this time, Egypt is the most powerful **empire** in the ancient world. A visit during the reign of Amenhotep II is highly recommended. Ancient Egyptian art is at its all-time best. You can admire the wall paintings, sculptures, and beautifully decorated jewelry. Many of these works of art are buried with the dead. You'll be able to sneak a peek before they are sealed away from human eyes for thousands of years.

WHEN NOT TO TRAVEL

- During the first intermediate period, when Egypt is shaken by war, national unrest, **plague**, and (later) foreign invasion.
- In the second intermediate period when the **Hyksos** have taken control of parts of ancient Egypt.
- By the third intermediate period and the late period, much of ancient Egypt has been ruled by the **Assyrians**, the **Persians**, the Libyans, the Nubians, and the Greeks.

Ramesses II ("The Great") (1279–1213 BC) was a strong ruler of the New Kingdom. His reign would be another good time to visit.

GEOGRAPHY AND CLIMATE

The Nile River dominates the landscape of ancient Egypt. It flows northward for more than 600 miles (965 kilometers) before it spreads out to form a **delta**. The land next to the river is beautiful and green. From high up, the delta looks like the back of a triangular leaf covered with veins. These veins are really hundreds of streams and water channels flowing into the blue-green Mediterranean Sea.

RED AND BLACK LAND

The ancient Egyptians call the lush strip of land surrounding the Nile *Kemet*, or "Black Land." It is named after the rich black **silt** that is washed up by the Nile when it floods each year. They call the desert beyond *Deshret*, or "Red Land." The change from fertile land to desert is rather sudden. It is even possible to put one foot on the "Black Land" and the other on the "Red Land."

LAND OF THE NILE
The Greek historian Herodotus (about 484–425 BCE) said "Egypt is the gift of her river."

THE SEASONS OF THE NILE

The Nile even makes the seasons. From July to October the fields surrounding the Nile are flooded. The farmers can't work on the flooded fields, so they find other work instead. Some of them work as builders. From November to February the farmers are back in the fields. You will see them busily ploughing and sowing. From March to June the farmers harvest their crops. This is the best time to sample fresh fruit and vegetables.

TEMPERATURES IN THE NILE VALLEY
July/August: temperature is between 77–104 °F (25–40 °C).
January: the coolest month with temperatures between 46–75 °F (8–24 °C).
There is little rainfall all over the country, but expect a few drops in winter around the Nile Delta.

Most of ancient Egypt's population is found on the **fertile** land surrounding the Nile. The people rely on the river for drinking water, agriculture, fish, trade, and communication.

GOOD NILE OR BAD NILE?

You will often hear the locals talk about a "good Nile" or a "bad Nile." They are talking about how good the floods have been. A "good Nile" means that the Nile has flooded the fields along its banks and there will be a good harvest. If it's a "bad Nile," then perhaps the river didn't flood. This could mean that the farmers don't have enough water for their crops and there may be famine.

CUSTOMS AND CULTURE

"GOD-KING"

Most rulers in ancient Egypt are men called pharaohs, but there are some queens, such as Queen Hatshepsut. Egyptians think the pharaoh is a descendent of the early gods. They believe he has control over everyday things, such as the flooding of the Nile. It is the custom in ancient Egypt to kiss the ground the pharaoh has walked on!

GOVERNMENT

The pharaoh has complete control over the running of the country. Second to the pharaoh is a kind of prime minister, called a **vizier**. He is the pharaoh's advisor, but he also acts as treasurer, **high priest**, and **chief justice**. There also is a whole network of officials who run different departments of government.

WHAT DO YOU CALL THE PHARAOH?

If you happen to meet the pharaoh, it is polite to call him "your majesty." During the period of the New Kingdom, people called the king *pr-aa*, which means "great house." This is where the word *pharaoh* comes from.

CLASS SYSTEM

At the top of the class system in ancient Egypt are the pharaoh and royal family. Next there are the **aristocracy** and other important people, such as the vizier. Government officials and priests also rank highly.

The pharaohs of ancient Egypt wear a false beard. It helps make them look intelligent and wise.

Next come administrators, **scribes**, and rich land owners. The largest part of society comes at the bottom and includes, in order of importance, soldiers, skilled and manual workers, peasant farmers, servants, and slaves. People don't complain about their position, as they believe that the gods decide a person's place in society.

WOMEN

Women from important or wealthy families in ancient Egypt have many rights. They can inherit property, run businesses, and become priestesses. People believe that the mother and wife of the pharaoh are divine and should be treated with respect.

A scribe uses a reed and a palette for writing. They usually use red and black ink.

However, women from lower on the social scale are treated as second-class citizens. They are expected to obey their husband and give him lots of children. Many women stay at home and run the household. Some women do work outside the home, acting as servants or doing jobs like weaving, baking, brewing, and farming.

CHILDREN

Families in ancient Egypt like to have lots of children. Only the boys of wealthy families go to school. Many children have to work. They often help their parents with farming, weaving, and brewing.

Children can marry in ancient Egypt. Girls often marry as young as 12 years old, and boys get married at 14 years old. This is because life expectancy is very short in ancient Egypt. Most people don't expect to live much longer than 40 years.

RELIGION

Religion is very important to ancient Egyptians. They worship many different gods and goddesses. They believe the gods have power over everything, including the size of this year's harvest, the weather, and the sex of a newborn baby.

KEEPING THE BALANCE

One of the most important parts of the religion of ancient Egyptians is about keeping order and balance in the universe. Ancient Egyptians believe the universe is made up of many opposites, such as birth and death, flooding and drought, and order and chaos. Most ancient Egyptians are very afraid of chaos. They believe that it is their responsibility to keep balance within the world.

A colorful **papyrus** called the Dendara Zodiac shows many of the gods and goddesses of ancient Egypt.

PLEASING MA'AT

The goddess of Universal Order is Ma'at. The pharaoh pleases Ma'at by performing rituals to all the gods at the temple each day. Everybody else pleases Ma'at by keeping balance in their lives, obeying the pharaoh, and being honest and just.

A GOD FOR EVERYTHING

There are more than 2,000 gods in ancient Egypt. The gods can be in human or animal form, or a strange mixture of both! There are national gods, which means they are worshipped by people all over the country. A popular national god is the sun god Re (or Amun-Re). On wall-paintings Re is usually shown as a falcon, a ram, or a man with a falcon or ram's head. There also are many local gods that are worshipped by people living in one area.

OTHER GODS TO LOOK OUT FOR...

- **Anubis** – The god of **mummification** (see page 16–17). He watches over priests as they **embalm** dead bodies. In art he is represented by a jackal or a man with a jackal's head.
- **Hathor** – Goddess of love, children, music, and dance. In pictures she is usually shown as a cow.
- **Horus** – The ancient god of the sky and the son of Osiris and Isis. Horus is usually represented by a falcon.
- **Osiris** – Husband and brother of Isis, and god of the underworld. In art he appears in human form with a crown of reeds and ostrich feathers, carrying a crook and flail.
- **Thoth** – The god of wisdom and the moon. On paintings he appears as an ibis or baboon.
- **Isis** – The greatest goddess of all, and the mother of Horus. She is the guardian of children and has amazing magical powers. In art she appears as a woman.

Horus

Osiris

Thoth

TEMPLES

Temples are not places where you can go to worship. These magnificent buildings are believed to be the home of the god to whom it is dedicated. A statue of the god is kept inside the **inner chamber**, the most holy part of the temple. The temples are run by priests and priestesses who perform special ceremonies and rituals to the god each day. Some temples are dedicated to the honor of a dead ruler.

Ordinary people are not allowed inside any of these temples. However, the buildings are truly impressive from the outside, so they are certainly worth a visit. The most outstanding temple complexes can be found at Karnak and Luxor (see pages 38–39).

This is an ancient Egyptian amulet with the Eye of Horus. People wear charms like this to protect them from evil.

WAYS OF WORSHIP

The outside walls of some temples are decorated with the ears of the god to whom they are dedicated. These are called chapels of the hearing ear. If you see people whispering into temple walls, it may look odd, but they are simply saying their prayers into the ear of the god.

Others worship by visiting small shrines dedicated to a certain god. You will see these **shrines** everywhere with offerings of food, flowers, and gifts. Ordinary people also make small shrines at home. These can be dedicated to the gods or to the spirit of a family member who has died.

MAGIC MOMENTS

The ancient Egyptians believe in magic. When a woman is going to have a baby, she chants spells to the gods Bes, Taweret, and Hathor, asking them to protect her and the baby. People also wear magic charms or **amulets** to ward off sickness and evil.

ANCIENT MUMMIES

The ancient Egyptians want to continue living forever. They believe that a corpse should be preserved for the **afterlife**. Ordinary people are usually laid to rest in the desert, where their body is dried by the sand and naturally **mummified**. They are then buried with some possessions (food, jewelry, amulets) they may need in the next life.

Royalty and the **elite** are mummified in a different way. The process of mummification takes 70 days from the moment of death. First of all, the lungs, stomach, liver, and intestines are removed. Then the corpse is packed with special salt. When the body is dried out, the salt is removed and the corpse is stuffed with resin and linen. Afterward, the body is covered in oil and perfume. Finally, the corpse is wrapped in linen bandages and laid to rest in a large stone coffin called a **sarcophagus**. The coffin is sealed away in a tomb with food and belongings, such as furniture, fine clothes, and jewelry that the person will need in the afterlife.

A tomb painting shows the god of mummification, Anubis (the jackal god), performing a ritual during the burial of a pharaoh.

This painted decoration from an 18th dynasty nobleman's tomb shows servants bearing offerings of geese, corn, and fine wine.

CHAPTER 2

PRACTICAL INFORMATION

Egypt is very hot, so you need to pack the right kinds of clothes for your visit. If you don't want to stand out in the crowd, then take lots of white clothing. On the food front, there are delicious fresh fruit and vegetables to sample, as well as the national dish of goose. And everyone drinks beer, including children! On a practical note, the ancient Egyptians don't use money, so read on to find out how you are going to make the most of your shopping trips.

WHAT TO WEAR

The ancient Egyptians have hardly changed the way they dress for thousands of years! They have always worn white linen, as it is lightweight and feels cool.

All men wear a kind of apron or kilt. It can be tied at the front or with two knots on either hip. In later times it is fashionable to wear pleated kilts with fringe at the edges. Men also usually wear a kind of tunic-style shirt.

Women look elegant in their straight sheath-like dresses, which are tied behind the neck or at each shoulder. On cool evenings most women wear a shawl. Slaves and servants sometimes wear clothes made from patterned fabric. Children dress much like their parents, or they wear nothing at all. People mostly go barefoot, but the rich sometimes wear sandals made of leather or reeds.

JEWELRY

Ancient Egyptian jewelry is colorful and eye-catching. People wear jeweled rings, anklets, bracelets, earrings, necklaces, collars, belts, and headdresses. The very rich can afford precious metals and jewels, but the poor make do with pottery beads. The ancient Egyptians make some of the most striking jewelry in the ancient world, which makes it an ideal gift to take home to loved ones.

This is a fine example of a precious amulet. At the center is the scarab beetle, said to symbolize rebirth.

FINISHING TOUCHES

The ancient Egyptians spend a lot of time trying to look good. Make-up isn't just for women—men use it, too. Most people use a black dye called kohl as eye-liner. Then they apply eye shadow—powdered malachite (a bright-green mineral) is very popular.

An ancient Egyptian girl with a woven wig. Beeswax is used to set the style.

Wigs are very popular among the upper classes. They help protect people from sunstroke. Women's hairstyles tend to be long and straight. Braids and jewels are sometimes added. Many people also shave off all their body hair. Children have short hair, often with a sidelock (a long lock of hair) on the righthand side of their head.

If you want to be fashionable in ancient Egypt, then wearing white is a must.

BE CLEOPATRA FOR A DAY!

A great way to relax is to have a full ancient Egyptian makeover. Start your pampering with a bath. Servants will pour jugs of water or milk over your skin. Next you will be covered in perfumed oil—this helps protect you from the sun. Then you can have your head shaved. The ancient Egyptians have excellent bronze razors. A special treatment for balding men is a scalp rub with snake or crocodile fat. Afterward, your eyes will be made up with kohl and eye shadow, and your lips and nails will be dyed with bright red henna (a dye from plant leaves). Finally, you'll be able to choose a wig from a selection made from human hair or plant fibers.

WHAT TO EAT

Ancient Egyptian food is very healthy. You'll find plenty of fresh fruit, onions, green vegetables, fish, and lentils on the menu, and not much fat or sugar.

The basis of all meals is bread—the ancient Egyptians were the first civilization to use yeast to make their bread rise. Most people eat a kind of bread made without yeast called unleavened bread. It is similar to pita bread. There are also delicious sweet breads that taste more like cake, such as bread sweetened with dates.

The ancient Egyptians use a selection of herbs and spices in their cooking, including rosemary, cinnamon, dill, cumin, and coriander. If you have a sweet tooth, then honey is used instead of sugar.

In this model, bakers are hard at work kneading dough to make bread.

ROAST PELICAN AND PIGEON

Meat is a delicacy and is expensive. The national dish is goose roasted over hot embers. It is usually eaten on special occasions, and then only by the rich or **elite**. Roast duck, beef, pigeon, and pelican also are popular. Pork is not a popular dish because some ancient Egyptians believe that pig meat carries **leprosy**. Meat and fish are often smoked or salted to preserve them.

WHAT TO DRINK

The water from the Nile can be brown and dirty, and is probably full of germs. But most local people drink it and survive to tell the tale. Beer is very popular, and people often brew it at home, using barley or wheat. Ancient Egyptian beer is very different from the beer people drink today. It is thick, like a milkshake, and is supposed to be really good for you.

The ancient Egyptians make their own wine, but there is also fine **imported** wine. Look for labels telling you about the wine—they tend to have no-nonsense descriptions such as "good wine," "very very good wine," and "sweet wine" written on them. Also, try the selection of freshly squeezed fruit juices.

The Nile Valley is perfect for growing grapes. These are often used to make delicious local wine.

TABLE MANNERS

Most ancient Egyptians eat squatting on the ground or on mats. Don't worry about using utensils, though. They use their fingers to eat, and pour water over their hands after each course of the meal. Wealthy Egyptians often sit on low chairs or cushions next to small tables.

MONEY

If you visit during the New Kingdom, you will find that the ancient Egyptians do not use money. (Money is introduced by the Greeks during the Ptolemaic period: 332–330 BCE.)

Usually, a person's wealth is measured by the number of cattle he or she owns. But don't panic—you won't need to take cattle with you all the way to ancient Egypt! Ancient Egyptians happily accept gold, other precious metals, grain, and oil in exchange for goods and services. Some people also take cloth, jewelry, or everyday objects. Remember to pack some things from home that are not available in ancient Egypt, as these will be excellent for **bartering**.

PRICES

As there is no money, it is difficult to give things a price. The ancient Egyptians price things by using copper weights or rings, called *debens* and *seniu*. If you're traveling during the New Kingdom, you will also find gold, silver, and copper weights called *kits*. Obviously, prices will vary depending on the period that you visit. During the New Kingdom, a sack of wheat weighing about 128 pounds (58 kilograms) is about two *deben* of copper. By the end of the period, during the reign of Ramesses XI, the value of an ox is about 5 kit of silver (or 60 *deben* of copper).

THE POSTAL SERVICE

Ancient Egyptians use symbols called **hieroglyphs** for writing. Scribes will take down your message on papyrus. The ancient Egyptians use messengers and soldiers to carry messages. They also have started a carrier pigeon service, in which messages are flown by specially trained pigeons. Whatever method you choose, don't expect the service to be quick! The best way of sending a message in ancient Egypt is via the Nile and then by horseback.

The grain harvested by hard-working slaves could be exchanged for other goods.

PAPERWORK

The ancient Egyptians love their paperwork. Scribes scribble away all day on papyrus, clay tablets, or wall paintings. They enjoy writing memos, letters, journals, wills, lists of rules and regulations, journals, transcripts of meetings, and trials from the law courts. The ancient Egyptians are very organized. If you travel in the New Kingdom, expect to be delayed on your journey by filling in lots of forms.

PAPYRUS FOR PAPER

Papyrus is a tough, tall river reed that you will see growing along the banks of the Nile. The ancient Egyptians have found a way of crushing the stems to make a kind of paper called papyrus. It is light and easier to transport than blocks of stone or clay. Papyrus reeds are also used to make sandals, boats, and rope.

A sailboat is the best way to travel in ancient Egypt.

CHAPTER 3

TRAVEL, FOOD, AND SHELTER

Most ancient Egyptians live near the Nile, and they get around by boat. You can expect to travel the same way on your visit, although horses are available if you can afford it. When it comes to places to stay in ancient Egypt, you will be relying on the hospitality of the locals.

If you're lucky you might get a room for the night. Otherwise, you may get a blanket and a place to sleep on the roof under the stars.

TRAVELING BY BOAT

The best way to travel between the major settlements along the Nile is, of course, by boat. And it is a wonderful experience! Boats traveling southward use sails. The power of the north wind blows the sails and powers the boats upriver, against the current. Boats going north let the river do the work, although oars are usually needed to steer them.

This barge is carrying a brightly painted shrine as part of a funeral ceremony.

Pharaohs and members of the royal family travel in magnificent barges. These have curved hulls and large, billowing rectangular sails. There are benches for the teams of oarsmen. These barges look majestic as they cut through the muddy waters of the Nile.
If you plan to travel in style, then this is the way to go.

HIEROGLYPHS TO REMEMBER

The picture of a ship with its sails billowing means "traveling south." The picture of a ship without a sail or mast means "traveling north."

RUSH HOUR ON THE NILE

If you are on a budget, then the ancient Egyptians have excellent riverboats. These are mostly made from papyrus, so they are light and glide through the water quickly. The river can get fairly busy carrying people and cargo. On your journeys you'll probably see plenty of big wooden barges carrying sculptures or large blocks of granite.

TRAVELING BY LAND

With the world's longest river flowing the length of the country, there hasn't been a great rush to build a network of roads in ancient Egypt. For trips overland farmers and peasants tend to use donkeys and **mules**, while the aristocracy often rides horses. Don't expect to see any camels until about 525 BCE, when the Persians invade and introduce this trusty animal.

If you have a lot of luggage, then try to visit after the second intermediate period (after 1550 BCE), by which time the wheeled **chariot** has been invented. Then at least you will be able to hire a cart.

A pharaoh and groom sit on a chariot pulled by a pony.

WHERE TO STAY

In ancient Egypt many people have an open-door policy, which means they will invite you to stay in their home. Of course, there is a big difference between a peasant's humble home and an aristocrat's luxury residence.

BUDGET BED AND BREAKFAST

Houses for workers and farmers are usually built of mud brick. They are built close together, sometimes in rows. You may be invited to sleep in a small room or even one of the storerooms. You'll probably have nothing more than a mat to sleep on.

Cooking takes place on the roof or in an unroofed room. If you are lucky there may be a toilet, which is a hole in the floor. The contents might be buried in a pit—otherwise they are dumped in the Nile. If there are no toilets, then there may be a pot, or you'll need to find a hidden spot outside!

This model of an ordinary ancient Egyptian house is called a soul house. It is home for a spirit in the afterlife.

FIVE-STAR ACCOMMODATION

If this sounds too uncomfortable, then try to get an invitation to a bigger house. These are often painted white to deflect the heat. They usually have walled gardens with trees and a pond. Inside, there are rooms for entertaining, cooking, and sleeping, as well as the servant's quarters and women's quarters.

Guests mostly stay on the first floor, while the owners stay on the floor above. The beds are made from wood and reeds, and are raised from the ground (away from the bugs!). Wooden headrests are provided instead of pillows.

At the best homes there are bathrooms, and servants give showers by pouring jugfuls of water over you. The toilets are not too bad—they consist of a wooden or stone seat on a small platform above a pot. Windows and roof vents are positioned to take full advantage of the cooling north winds.

BOOK A TRIP TO AN OASIS

For the more adventurous there are **caravan** routes through the desert to the major **oases**. It takes weeks to reach one of these lush outposts. On the way you'll be camping out under the stars or in simple tents made from reeds and rough linen. Once you arrive, you will be rewarded with excellent boating, swimming, fishing, and hunting. But watch out for hungry crocodiles and angry hippos!

The mysterious Sphinx watches over the great pyramids at Giza. It has a human head and a lion's body.

CHAPTER 4

PLACES TO VISIT

There are many wonderful places to visit in ancient Egypt. Most people who visit ancient Egypt think about the pyramids first, so a trip to Giza is a must for everyone. Some people can't wait to see the magnificent temples at Karnak, near Thebes. Don't let the fact that Giza and Thebes are hundreds of miles apart make you think twice about visiting both of them. Actually, it's pretty easy to plan a trip that takes in most of the major tourist sites in ancient Egypt. Nearly all of them are along the Nile, so it's possible to sail upriver (or paddle downriver!). You can stop along the way and encounter all the treasures that ancient Egypt has to offer. Remember, you will have to barter with local boatmen, so take plenty of useful goods like fine cloth, jewels, and precious metal!

THE ROYAL CITY OF MEMPHIS

Memphis is a fashionable and exciting capital city located on the west bank of the Nile. It is a sprawling city that measures 18.6 miles (30 kilometers) from north to south. It is also a wonder of early engineering. The city is built on land that used to be flooded by the Nile. Now man-made **dykes** protect it from rising waters.

For an unusual day out you could visit the bird breeding grounds on the Memphis lakes. You'll see birds such as the ibis and falcon. When they are fully grown, these birds will be mummified. The ancient Egyptians place mummified birds and animals in their tombs to keep them company in the afterlife.

This amazing decorated tomb of a vizier named Mereruka can be found in Saqqara.

TOP ATTRACTIONS IN MEMPHIS

- The Palace of Apries: impressive courtyard, throne room with beautiful limestone columns.
- The Temple of Ptah: you won't be able to see inside, but it has a splendid **hypostyle** hall with rows of stone columns.
- Fine parks, gardens, and lakes found around the city.

CITY OF THE DEAD

A trip to Saqqara and Giza is the highlight of a visit to ancient Egypt. Saqqara and Giza are known as "the city of the dead," or **necropolis**. There are cemeteries, tombs, temples, and of course, the pyramids, where the bodies of the dead pharaohs are laid to rest. The huge sloping sides of the pyramids are built as stairways to the sun for the pharaohs. The structures are solid except for a few chambers (rooms) where the body of the pharaoh and his belongings rest.

THE GREAT PYRAMID

A good time to visit is during the reign of Khufu of the Old Kingdom (2589–2566 BCE). He is building the Great Pyramid at Giza as a stronghold for his body and a monument of his reign. His own mother's grave has been robbed, so he plans to make his Great Pyramid impossible to raid.

THE FIRST PYRAMID

Between the third and twelfth dynasties (2686–1795 BCE), about 80 pyramids were built. The first pyramid to be built was the step pyramid at Saqqara. It gets its name because its sides look like six giant steps. It was built for Pharaoh Djoser by his **architect** and vizier, Imhotep (see also page 56), around 2660 BCE.

You will be able to see how the workers haul large chunks of stone across the desert using wooden rollers. When the Great Pyramid is finished, it is called one of the seven wonders of the ancient world, so seeing how it is built is an opportunity not to be missed!

A TRIP DOWN THE NILE VALLEY

BENI HASAN

It is best to visit the necropolis Beni Hasan during the Middle Kingdom (2055–1650 BCE), when the local rulers are building some especially beautiful tombs. The tomb of Khnumhotep II, a local governor, has some of the most famous art in ancient Egypt, with many beautiful paintings of daily life. Meanwhile, at the tomb of Kheti, you will see paintings of farming and wine-making.

THE ART OF THE WALL-PAINTER

This wall painting from the tomb of Khnumhotep II shows a slave harvesting figs. Ancient Egyptians have wall painting down to a fine art. First of all, stonemasons smooth the walls and apply a layer of plaster. Next, the wall is divided into a grid using red paint. Then the scribes copy their sketched designs onto the walls using black paint. Next, the stonemasons chip out the important images, so they stand out from the background. Last of all, the painters fill in the colors. The bright greens are made from powdered malachite. The deep red is made from iron oxide mixed with egg white and gum.

AKHETATEN

The city of Akhetaten was created for the New Kingdom ruler Amenhotep IV (1352–1336 BCE), who started a new religion based on worshipping the god of the sun disc, Aten. As part of the new religion, Amenhotep changed his name to Akhenaten and built a city dedicated to Aten. However, this caused religious upheaval because most ancient Egyptians believe in many gods.

Akhetaten is only the capital city during the reign of King Akhenaten, so you have just fourteen years to visit! The city has many interesting sites. Unlike most other temples, the Great Temple of Aten has no roof, so sunlight floods into the temple.

Other attractions include the king's beautiful wife Nefertiti. Rumor has it she is one of the most beautiful women in ancient Egypt. She is certainly one of the most powerful women, and you would be lucky to get a glimpse of her.

A famous face: Queen Nefertiti and her daughter worship the sun god Aten.

ABYDOS

Abydos is a holy place in ancient Egypt and the center of worship to the god of the dead, Osiris. You will see many people making a pilgrimage to the Temple of Osiris. Ancient Egyptians try to visit Abydos once in their lifetime. A good time to visit is during the Abydos Festival, which is held once a year. You will see plays of the story of Isis and Osiris, and pageants and processions. The town comes alive with celebration and excitement.

THEBES

Thebes is the capital city of the New Kingdom. It's like two towns in one city. On the east bank of the Nile is the thriving commercial city and the stunning temples of Karnak and Luxor. The west bank of the Nile is very different—it's a barren place with dry limestone hills. These dusty hilltops are the burial ground for the New Kingdom pharaohs. It is called the Valley of the Kings.

This is a view across the sacred lake of Amun, Karnak.

THE MAGIC OF KARNAK

You will need a few days to take in all the wonderful sites on the east bank of Thebes and the temples at Karnak. Together, they form the largest temple complex in ancient Egypt. The three temple complexes include the temple to the god Amun, king of the gods, and two smaller temples dedicated to the gods Mut and Khonsu.

The Temple of Amun is approached from the Nile by an impressive avenue of **sphinxes** with rams' heads. The temple walls are decorated with painted scenes of everyday and religious life. Inside the temple, watch for the impressive **colossus** of Ramesses II. This giant granite statue stands at the entrance to the Great Hypostyle Hall. It was built by Sety I and finished by Ramesses II, so it might be best to plan your trip once Ramesses has completed it.

LUXOR

Luxor Temple is just 1.2 miles (2 kilometers) from Karnak. You can reach it by river, or you might walk along the elegant avenue of sphinxes, which connect Karnak and Luxor. Luxor is also dedicated to the gods Amun, Mut, and Khonsu. It is much smaller than Karnak but has some equally interesting sites. At the entrance of the temple are two statues of Ramesses II. There is also a striking pair of pink granite obelisks. These reach 82 feet (25 meters) into the air and point toward the sun god Re.

THE FESTIVAL OF OPET

If you want to see the ancient Egyptians letting their hair down, then head for Karnak during the Festival of Opet. The festival celebrates the king's rebirth as the son of Amun and takes place each year during the floods. Crowds of people line the banks of the Nile to watch the sacred statue of Amun being taken upriver by boat from Karnak to the temple at Luxor. Later, the pharaoh takes part in a special ceremony and everyone celebrates his god-like status.

The Sphinxes at Luxor. The human head represents intelligence, and the lion's body symbolizes strength.

INTO THE VALLEY OF THE KINGS

Plan your day out at the Valley of the Kings for the early morning or late afternoon, when the Sun is less bright. Take plenty of water and pack a scarf to protect yourself from the sun. The dry limestone hills in the Valley of the Kings aren't welcoming, but this is why the pharaohs chose this place to be buried. They wanted somewhere remote, far away from grave robbers and other people, where they could truly rest in peace.

This is the death mask of Tutankhamen, buried within a tomb in the Valley of the Kings.

The Valley of the Kings is supposed to be a secret place. If you want to catch a glimpse of the treasures being taken to the tombs, then plan your trip during the New Kingdom (1550–1069 BCE) when the tombs are being built. Highlights include the tomb of Ramesses VI. It has a large arched roof that is decorated with the goddess Nut swallowing the sun. The tomb of the boy-king Tutankhamen is also worth a visit. His mummy is covered with a beautiful golden mask, and he is buried with mountains of gold and precious jewels, childhood toys, baskets of fruit, and jars of wine.

This is one of the two sentinels who guard the entrance to Tutankhamen's burial chambers.

At Deir-al-Bahn in Luxor stands the temple of Queen Hatshepsut, one of the few female Egyptian pharaohs. Much of the temple is destroyed by Ramesses II, so plan a trip there before his reign.

TOP TOMBS

The Valley of the Kings has hundreds of tombs that have been cut into the cliffs. Some of these are very deep with stairs, hallways leading to burial chambers. A few tombs have false burial chambers to trick tomb robbers. Most of the tombs are decorated with wall-paintings that show the journey to the Afterlife. Nobles and other important people are also buried near the Valley of the Kings.

VALLEY OF THE QUEENS

Royal wives and children are laid to rest in the Valley of the Queens. It is rumored that the most beautiful tomb in all ancient Egypt has been built here for Queen Nefertari, the favorite wife of Ramesses II. Wonderful wall-paintings show Nefertari on her journey to the afterlife.

HOMES FOR THE WORKERS

A visit to Thebes would not be complete without a quick peek at Deir el-Medina. This new town has been built to house the builders and families of people working at the Valley of the Kings. It is cleverly designed, with streets of rowhouses, shops, and businesses. There is also a fine temple dedicated to Hathor.

This colorful wall painting shows the nobleman Nebamun as he hunts for birds and fish on the Nile.

CHAPTER 5

THINGS TO DO

There's more to ancient Egypt than temples and tombs. Once you've gone sightseeing, you might want to do some shopping. There are plenty of opportunities to grab a few bargains at the market place. The ancient Egyptians head for the Nile to swim, fish, and hunt. For your entertainment there are banquets with dancers, acrobats, and musicians. There are also plays at the temples and hockey matches in the towns. Highlights of the year are the festivals, such as the festival of Bastet, when all the locals parade in the street.

LET'S SHOP!

The marketplaces of ancient Egypt are filled with fresh fish, fruit and vegetables, herbs and spices, and a delicious assortment of home-baked bread and home-brewed beer. If you're looking for local handicrafts, then it may be better to visit local craftspeople. You should be able to find potters, carpenters, glassmakers, jewelers, weavers, and leatherworkers going about their business in most major towns.

BARTERING FOR BEGINNERS

If you're used to buying things with money, then bartering for goods might feel a bit strange. It's good to have a rough idea of the value of the goods you wish to buy before you begin your shopping trip. Stallholders at the market usually weigh their produce using copper weights called *debens*. If you have a piece of linen worth one deben, then it can be exchanged for goods worth one deben. With craftspeople it will be a matter of bargaining until you can agree on an exchange you are both happy with.

The ancient Egyptians have a wide selection of interesting board games. Some are made in the shapes of animals, like this one.

WHAT TO BUY?

If you want a typically ancient Egyptian souvenir, then why not
choose a board game like Senet (see box) or Hounds and Jackals?
There also are some lovely toys, such as carved ivory animals, dolls,
wooden animals (look out for crocodiles and leopards with mouths
that snap shut), boats, and balls. You could also buy polished
bronze or copper mirrors, fine linen, perfume oils, glassware,
statuettes of gods and goddesses, and musical instruments.

BEAUTIFUL JEWELRY

Ancient Egyptian jewelry is
beautiful to look at and has
hidden meaning, too. People
believe that certain precious
jewels, gemstones, and metals
can protect or bring good luck
to the wearer. Lapis lazuli
(a bright blue gemstone) and
turquoise (a greenish-blue
semi-precious stone) are
thought to bring joy and

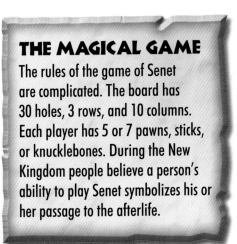

THE MAGICAL GAME

The rules of the game of Senet
are complicated. The board has
30 holes, 3 rows, and 10 columns.
Each player has 5 or 7 pawns, sticks,
or knucklebones. During the New
Kingdom people believe a person's
ability to play Senet symbolizes his or
her passage to the afterlife.

delight. Gold is connected to the sun, and copper is associated with
the goddess Hathor. Note that silver is rarer than gold, so it is more
expensive. Glass beads are also very popular.

A LASTING MEMORY

Why not ask an artist to capture you or your family on papyrus?
Ancient Egyptian artists have their own style. They paint eyes and
shoulders as if they were seeing the person from the front and they
paint the body from the side, as in the picture on page 42.

TAKE ME TO THE RIVER

When it comes to having a good time, the Nile provides endless possibilities. There is excellent swimming and boating. Boat races and boat games are also popular. One game, in which two teams of men holding long poles attempt to push each other into the river, causes a big splash! Fishing is common, as is hunting birds with throw-sticks (these are similar to extra-large boomerangs), and crocodile and hippopotamus hunting can be arranged.

Slave girls entertain guests at a banquet with music and dancing.

There is hunting inland, too. In the desert people trap animals such as hares, hyenas, gazelles, and foxes. If you travel to ancient Egypt from the time of the New Kingdom (1550–1069 BCE), big-game hunting on chariots is also popular.

ENTERTAINMENT

Plays are sometimes performed at the temples. These plays are about religion and are nothing like the theater you may have seen. People also enjoy watching a kind of ball game that is similar to hockey. Men use long palm tree branches for sticks and have a puck (hard disc) made from leather stuffed with papyrus.

LAVISH BANQUETS

Ancient Egyptian banquets are a must for any traveler. Most banquets are private parties hosted by the middle and upper classes. There is plenty of entertainment, with music, singing, dancing, jugglers, and acrobats. Servants will bring you the finest selection of food, and your cup will be filled regularly with wine or beer. The ancient Egyptians like to get drunk and are regularly sick from too much alcohol.

FESTIVALS

The ancient Egyptian word for a party or holy day (holiday) is *heru-nefer*, which translates as "a good day." Festivals and holidays are an excuse for rich and poor to eat and drink too much and to enjoy music and dancing. The festivals to the lesser gods tend to be less serious and more fun. On the holy day of the cat goddess Bastet, no work is done and people parade in the streets wearing masks. The Beautiful Feast of the Valley is celebrated each year in Thebes. The highlight of the day is visiting the tombs of loved ones and eating a meal at the graveside.

HOW STRANGE!

At some parties, servants put cones of perfumed grease on the heads of the guests. As the grease melts, it runs down onto the guest's hair and face. This is supposed to cool the person down!

A nobleman, dressed in a panther skin, offers lotus and papyrus to the god Osiris.

The Eye of Horus regularly appears on wall paintings or as an amulet. This protects people from evil and illness.

CHAPTER 6

HEALTH AND SAFETY

If you get ill in ancient Eygpt, then you'd better believe in magic! People practice **faith healing**, cast spells, or pray to the gods for a cure. However, the ancient Egyptians do know quite a lot about the human body and how it works. And they have some of the best doctors in the ancient world. If you get into trouble with the law, you may be surprised by how fair the legal system can be. There is a police force and law courts with judges. There isn't much crime in ancient Egypt, but like anywhere you should be careful. Robbers do exist, although most of them would rather steal from a tomb than pick your pocket.

HEALTH – WHAT TO EXPECT

Stomach problems and diarrhea are common in ancient Egypt. Most vacationers get sick sometime during their visit. It's hardly surprising because people throw human waste outside their homes. Birds, animals, and insects feed on the rubbish and spread germs quickly. Eye infections and diseases are extremely common. Visitors can be badly affected by heat. Sunstroke and sunburn can ruin your vacation, so be careful in the sun and stay in the shade if possible.

DEADLY DISEASES OF ANCIENT EGYPT

- **Cholera**: waterborne disease causing severe diarrhea and vomiting.
- **Tuberculosis**: airborne disease that affects the lungs.
- **Smallpox**: highly contagious virus; causes spots on the skin that leave scars.
- **Bilharzia**: passed to humans by infected snails living in freshwater.
- **Malaria**: passed to humans by infected mosquitoes.

A VISIT TO THE DOCTOR

Ancient Egyptian doctors are possibly the best you will find in the ancient world. They know a lot about the human body and how it works. This knowledge probably comes from their experience of removing organs and embalming bodies for mummification. Ancient Egyptian surgeons have even attempted brain surgery.

However, the ancient Egyptians haven't quite mastered medicine. They think that the heart is used for thinking and don't know what the brain is used for. But don't let this worry you, as most doctors use their common sense. They only turn to magic and religion if they can't find a cure. Be prepared for a doctor to ask you some some strange questions, though. Many doctors believe that dreams can hold the answer to the state of your health.

FIGHTING SICKNESS

Medicine and treatments can be anything from very good to very odd. Eye infections are helped by applying a mixture of honey and ochre to the eyes using a vulture **quill** for a dropper. But it's probably best to avoid cures such as water from pigs' eyes or tortoise bile (digestive juices).

Honey is commonly used as an antiseptic to kill germs and bacteria, and it does seem to help minor cuts and wounds heal. Some doctors will apply raw meat to a bad wound, which they say helps stop the bleeding. Broken bones are set using wooden splints or palm ribs.

A doctor attends to a patient with an eye problem.

COMMON ANCIENT EGYPTIAN CURES
- **To stop diarrhea**: take one-eighth of a cup of figs and grapes, bread dough, corn, fresh earth, onion, and elderberry.
- **To cure indigestion**: crush a hog's tooth and put inside four sugar cakes. Eat one cake a day for four days.
- **To ease pain**: anoint the body (cover in oil) and expose to the sun.

SECURITY

Ancient Egypt is one of the safest places in the ancient world for travelers. People don't use money or carry wallets and purses, so there is little threat from pickpockets. As most of your travel is by boat on the Nile, you won't need to keep a lookout for bandits hiding in the hills. Ancient Egypt is also safe because people have strong religious beliefs (see pages 14–15). Most people try to be honest because that is the best way of pleasing the goddess Ma'at.

BEWARE OF THIEVES!

Even though you are fairly safe in ancient Egypt, it is best to be on your guard. Thieves may try to steal your luggage, and there will always be people who try to take advantage of you.

One of the biggest crimes in ancient Egypt is tomb robbery. This is so common that it is regarded as a profession. Tomb robbers usually work in teams and steal from royal tombs. They can take everything from the fine jewelry and precious items buried with the mummy to the gold fittings on the sarcophagus.

A TIME TO AVOID!

Don't travel to ancient Egypt during the first intermediate period [2181–2055 BCE]. Here is a news report from the day: "Behold, the land is full of gangs and the farmer goes to plough with his shield... crime is everywhere... wearers of fine linen are beaten with sticks... Behold, things are done that were never done before, and the king has been robbed by beggars." (From *The Admonitions of Ipuwer/ Judgement of the Pharaoh* by Joyce Tyldesley.)

↲ These men are being led off to be punished for not working hard enough!

PUNISHMENT

It takes a brave person to rob a royal tomb. He is disobeying the pharaoh and displeasing the gods. The penalty for this is high. The sentence for tomb robbery is death by impalement. This means that the guilty person is lowered onto a sharp stake and left to die very slowly. The robber is also so badly beaten that his body is no use to him in the afterlife (a terrible fate for any ancient Egyptian).

For petty crimes people are beaten, whipped, branded, or have their ears and nose cut off. The police and tax collectors regularly use leather batons and sticks, too. There are prisons, but ancient Egyptians prefer their punishments to be painful and quick.

Hieroglyphs are believed to be the first writing system in the world.

CHAPTER 7

ANCIENT EGYPT FACTS AND FIGURES

This final section is an easy reference guide for the time traveler. Check out "Ancient Egypt at a glance" to find out the major periods and royal dynasties of ancient Egypt. This chapter gives you a quick list of some of the royal figures and celebrities to look out for. No trip to a foreign land is complete without a phrase book. In ancient Egypt people use picture words called hieroglyphs. They are often beautiful to look at but can be very difficult to understand, so a selection of common words and their meanings is given in this section.

ANCIENT EGYPTIAN PHRASE BOOK

The ancient Egyptians use picture writing called hieroglyphs for tomb wall paintings and temples. There are several thousand hieroglyphs, so it is a difficult language to master. However, hieroglyphs are extremely beautiful, almost like works of art. The hieroglyphs can be read vertically and horizontally. Scribes also use a kind of shorthand of hieroglyphs called hieratic writing.

SOME COMMON EGYPTIAN HIEROGLYPHS

quail   owl   snake   water

jug   hand   foot

1   2   10   100   1,000

10,000   100,000   1,000,000

USEFUL EGYPTIAN WORDS AND PHRASES

(Pronunciation is in *italics*)

I = *inek*
my = say *ee* after the word
My name is … = *ren-ee* …

Hello = *hee*
Good morning = *sebat neferet*
Good evening = *masheru nefer*

Where (is…)? = *chen…?*
How much (is…)? = *wer…?*
I want, I would like = *mer-ee*

this = *pen*
that = *pef*
there = *im*

water = *mu*
bread = *ta*
figs = *daby*
fish = *rem*
meat = *iwef*
food = *wenemet*
eat = *wenem*
drink = *sewary*

I am/we are hungry = *inek/inu heker*
I am/we are thirsty = *inek/inu ibu*
chariot = *wereret*
to sail south = *henet*
to sail north = *hed*
to sail across = *wedja*
to go = *shem*
Do you go to… = *shem-tenu en*…

bad = *bin*
good = *nefer*
a little (of) = *nehy (en)*

one = *wat*
two = *senu*
ten = *medju*
many = *asha*

today = *hen*
tomorrow = *miseba*
yes = *chew*
no = *nen*

ANCIENT EGYPT AT A GLANCE

TIMELINE
(*Please note that dates are approximate.*)

5500–3000 BCE   PRE–DYNASTIC PERIOD
The beginning of hieroglyphic writing

3100–2686 BCE   EARLY DYNASTIC PERIOD
The creation of the Egyptian state in about 3250 BCE.

3100–2890	1st dynasty
3100	Narmer (Menes)
2890–2686	2nd dynasty

2686–2181 BCE   OLD KINGDOM
The Great Pyramids at Giza are built.

2686–2613	3rd dynasty
2686–2667	Sanakht
2667–2648	Djoser
2613–2498	4th dynasty
2613–2589	Sneferu
2589–2566	Khufu
2558–2532	Khafra
2494–2345	5th dynasty
2345–2181	6th dynasty

2181–2055 BCE   FIRST INTERMEDIATE PERIOD
Egypt is divided into two states, with a northern capital at Memphis and a southern capital at Thebes. (Thebes was the only capital during the 11th dynasty.)

2181–2125	7th and 8th dynasties
2160–2025	9th and 10th dynasties
2125–2055	11th dynasty

2055–1650 BCE   MIDDLE KINGDOM
The country is reunited by the pharaoh Mentuhotep II; the classical period of art and literature.

2055–1985	11th dynasty
2055–2004	Mentuhotep II
1985–1795	12th dynasty
1985–1955	Amenemhat I
1795–1650	13th and 14th dynasties

1650–1550 BCE   SECOND INTERMEDIATE PERIOD
15th, 16th and 17th dynasties. Dates from this period are uncertain. Ancient Egypt is ruled by the Hykos until Egyptian rulers drive them out and begin the 17th dynasty.

1550–1069 BCE   NEW KINGDOM
Often described as the golden age of ancient Egypt. The second half of the 18th dynasty and beginning of the 19th dynasty are a good time to visit ancient Egypt. Building work starts at the Valley of the Kings.

1550–1295	18th dynasty
	Ahmose
1525–1504	Amenhotep I
1473–1458	Queen Hatshepsut
1427–1400	Amenhotep II
1352–1336	Amenhotep IV (Akhenaten)
1336–1327	Tutankhamen
1323–1295	Horemheb
1295–1186	19th dynasty
1295–1294	Ramesses I
1294–1279	Sety I
1279–1213	Ramesses II
1186–1069	20th dynasty

1069–747 BCE   THIRD INTERMEDIATE PERIOD
Ancient Egypt loses power and is taken over by Nubian rulers. 21st, 22nd, 23rd, 24th dynasties rule the country.

747–332 BCE   LATE PERIOD
The Assyrians and Persians rule over ancient Egypt. 25th, 26th, 27th, 28th, 29th and 30th dynasties rule the country.

332–305 BCE   THE MACEDONIANS
Alexander the Greek conquers ancient Egypt in 332.

305–30 BCE   THE PTOLEMAIC DYNASTY
A troubled time which begins with the rule of Ptolemy I, a general of Alexander the Great.

51–30	Queen Cleopatra.
30	Egypt becomes part of the Roman Empire.

GREAT ANCIENT EGYPTIANS

- **Imhotep** (around 2675 BCE) – designed what was probably the first pyramid, the Step Pyramid at Saqqara (see page 35).
- **Khufu** (around 2589–2566 BCE) – a strong and possibly cruel leader, Khufu's kingdom was so strong that his country was never attacked from outside. Khufu is famous for building the Great Pyramid at Giza.
- **Tutankhamen** (died circa 1325 BCE) – became pharaoh when he was just nine years old. He died around age 18. Some people believe that he was murdered, but there is no proof.
- **Ramesses II** (circa 1279–1213 BCE) – also known as Ramesses the Great, this mighty pharaoh ruled ancient Egypt for 66 years. He was a military man who defeated the Hittites at the Battle of Qadesh in about 1274 BCE. His interest in building was well known. Among his finest buildings are the Great Temple at Abu Simbel, the colonnaded hall at the Karnak Temple, and the **mortuary** temple of his father Sety I at Thebes.

CLEOPATRA: THE LAST RULER OF ANCIENT EGYPT

Cleopatra VII (circa 51–30 BCE) took the throne at age 19, sharing it with her younger brother, Ptolemy XIII. However, Ptolemy plotted to rule Egypt without her, and Cleopatra was forced into exile. At the time, the Roman Empire was more powerful than Egypt, so Cleopatra made an alliance with a Roman general called Julius Caesar. Caesar drove Ptolemy out and Cleopatra regained her throne. Later, Cleopatra gave birth to Caesar's son, Caesarion, and visited him in Rome. Caesar was assassinated in 44 BCE, and Cleopatra returned to Egypt, ruling with her son.

In 41 BCE Cleopatra formed a relationship with the Roman leader Mark Antony. Mark Antony was to marry Cleopatra and live in Egypt. This made him unpopular at home, and in 32 BCE the Roman Empire declared war on Egypt. After losing a critical battle, Mark Antony committed suicide and Cleopatra was captured. She is said to have killed herself by getting an asp (a snake) to bite her. She was the last ruler of ancient Egypt before it became part of the mighty Roman Empire.

FURTHER READING

BOOKS

Day, Nancy. *Your Travel Guide to Ancient Egypt.* Minneapolis: Lerner Publishing Group, 2005

Harris, Nathaniel. *Everyday Life in Ancient Egypt.* North Mankato, MN: Sea-To-Sea Publications, 2005

Hodge, Susie. *Ancient Egyptian Art.* Chicago: Heinemann Library, 2006

Morgan, Julian. *Cleopatra: Ruling in the Shadow of Rome.* New York: Rosen Publishing Group, 2003

WEBSITES

- http://www.ancient-egypt.org/

- http://www.mnsu.edu/emuseum/prehistory/egypt/

GLOSSARY

afterlife place where ancient Egyptians believed the dead went

amulet good luck charm, often worn as jewelry

architect person who designs buildings

aristocracy highest social rank in society, the nobility

bartering trading by exchanging food or other goods rather than using money

capital most important city in a country. It is usually the center of government.

caravan number of travelers and camels crossing a desert together

chariot small, two-wheeled cart pulled by a horse or mule

chief justice leading judge in a court of law

colossus statue that is much bigger than life size

delta area where a river begins to spread out into several channels before it reaches the sea

dyke long wall or embankment that is built to stop flooding, especially from rivers or the sea

elite top rank of society

embalm treat a dead body with spices and oils to stop it from decaying

empire group of countries or lands that are controlled by one ruler

faith healing way of healing a person using faith and trust, often in religion, rather than medicine

fertile something that is rich and full of goodness. Fertile land is good for growing plants and crops

hieroglyph symbol or picture that is used in ancient Egyptian writing

high priest chief priest who worked in a temple serving the gods and goddesses

Hyksos group of foreign people, probably from Palestine or Syria

hypostyle great hall with a roof that is supported by rows of stone columns

imported brought foreign goods into another country

leprosy skin disease that can cause parts of skin and limbs to rot away

mortuary room or building where dead bodies are kept until they are buried

mule offspring of a female horse and a male donkey

mummification process of preserving a dead body by embalming and wrapping it in bandages

necropolis ancient cemetery or burial place

oasis fertile area in the desert with its own natural source of water

papyrus reed that the ancient Egyptians made into paper

plague deadly disease that spreads quickly over a wide area

quill hollow stem of a bird's feather, used as a pen

sarcophagus stone coffin that is often decorated with sculptures or carved inscriptions

scribe person whose job it is to copy books or documents by hand

shrine place that is sacred to a god or holy person

silt fertile mud washed up from the riverbed during floods

sphinx stone sculpture with a lion's body and a human head

vizier chief advisor to the pharaoh

INDEX